Journey to Zero

Ancient Meditation Techniques

Adapted For Modern Living

Milind Dhond

ISBN: 978-0-9964904-0-5

www.journeytozerobook.com

Cover & Graphic Design - Michael Clawson

Copy Editor - Kira Bohm

To Tessa and the "Guys" – Alex, Kailas, and Maya

Lata and Bapu

Special thanks to Dominic Uchikura

Jeff Frye, and Tyron Burnett

Michael and Patty Clawson

Table of Contents

How to use this book

In general, meditation is a life-long practice similar to physical exercise. It requires the allotting of specific time, ideally on a daily basis.

I would recommend finding a quiet place in the house that can be used for regular meditation. It should be quiet and comfortable to sit for 30-40 minutes.

Plan a specific time of day when you won't feel rushed for this activity.

Sit with a cushion underneath your backside so that your feet are on the ground and your backside is slightly elevated. This position will lean you forward slightly, allowing you to sit in a meditative posture for a longer period of time than if you were to sit on a flat surface.

If you cannot sit like this for some reason then you can sit in a chair with a straight back so that your spine is straight.

Read through the initial exercises in the book, such as techniques 1-2, so that you can picture the whole technique in your mind.

Sitting in a cross-legged posture on the cushion as described, put your hands in the respective mudra and then relax all your muscles, starting from the top of your head down to your feet.

Then begin practicing. Your general feeling should be one of relaxation. Your breaths should be relaxed and the suspension not so long that you feel short of breath.

Thoughts naturally creep into the meditation when you first start and you may find that you are daydreaming while doing the practice. This is normal and you should focus back on counting the numbers. The more you practice, the easier it will become to keep your mind still for longer.

You should focus initially on these first practices until you can make your mind still. Then try the others.

In general you will find some that work very well for you, while others have little or no effect. Stick with the ones that you feel benefit you the most.

There is no secret to meditation. If you practice sincerely over a period of time you will experience your mind becoming one-pointed. Once this occurs and it is silent then you will go deeper into the silence and "experience" the mystic states described in this book.

Background

The pursuit of spiritual knowledge is a difficult path that usually requires the guidance of a spiritual preceptor who has direct knowledge of the subject.

It cannot be learnt by merely reading a book or by intellectualization of the subject. It has to be experienced directly by the practitioner. The spiritual seeker often finds him- or herself driven by an unknown urge or desire to seek out this knowledge. The adage "when the student is ready the teacher will appear" pertains to those seeking this type of knowledge.

From a personal standpoint, I had long been perplexed as to why reading spiritual books gave me a feeling of exhilaration. The knowledge I obtained always seemed only theoretical and I was unable to directly experience the truth. I seemed to understand the general gist of the texts but was always stumped by unintelligible phrases and metaphors such as "It is beyond the known and the unknown." This left me with deep questions about what was needed to progress from intellectual knowledge to truth. Having spent many years meditating and hoping to experience the truth myself, I was fortunate enough to have Swami Radhikananda Saraswati from the

Siddha Yoga School in Pune, India show up at my house in California in 2003. It was during one of our meditation sessions that she asked if I wish to be initiated with a Diksha -- literally, a direct transmission of spiritual knowledge. The experience is described in detail later in this book. My subsequent journey was one of gradual awakening and realization of the truth. One of the biggest leaps in my pursuit occurred one day in August 2012, when Swamiji arrived for her annual session with our group in Davis, CA and announced that for the next ten days we would be deciphering an ancient Sanskrit yoga text entitled Vijnana Bhairava, or divine consciousness. The book, written in the 8th century, contains 112 techniques for attaining a state of Bhairava, literally a state of the divine. It was, as she described it, "the PhD of yogic meditational practice." The actual author of the text is unknown, but it was taught and interpreted by the yogic sages of that era, primarily Abhinavagupta. The book forms part of a larger text on yoga called the Rudrayamala Tantra, which has been lost. This type of meditational yoga forms part of a broader school of practice referred to as Kashmiri Shaivism.

The following work represents a distillation of the sessions with the Swami and my subsequent experiences and practice of the techniques.

The techniques have been written in a simple form that describes step by step how one can experience their effect. There is reference to the somewhat esoteric description of the techniques outlined in the original text itself.

The excellent English translation of Vijnana Bhairava by Jaidev Singh has been used as a reference and the reader would be aided by reading this if a deeper knowledge of the original work is desired.

Swami Radhikananda Saraswati

Swami Radhikananda Saraswati is the daughter of the renowned historian Padmabhushan Setu.

Swamiji was initiated by Swami Mukhtananda, and subsequently by her Guru, Swami Umananda. Swamiji plunged into spiritual 'sadhana' and founded the Sidha Yoga Ashram in Pune, India in 1987. Today, the Ashram is an abode where hundreds of seekers on the spiritual path find solace. Swami Radhikananda's unique contributions to society were acknowledged in 1997, when the title 'Dharmalankar' was conferred upon her. Swamiji is the author of numerous books on Kundalini Yoga, including Dnyaneshwari Once Again – a complete English translation of Dnyaneshwari's epic.

Om

Guruve namaha

shri guruve namaha

Introduction

For the purposes of this book I have defined truth as the direct, immediate, non-relational realization of the Divine.

The book does not presuppose any religious beliefs and can be applied to any preexisting philosophy as desired by the reader. The techniques and subsequent experiences stand alone.

The book has a Background Concepts section to help the reader with understanding the practices, and I have left the Sanskrit and Indian names, as this work is derived from a Yoga perspective. Yoga for this purpose means "union of the individual consciousness with the divine." I would recommend that the reader familiarize him- or herself with the background concepts and the types of practice involved with each technique before starting.

The practices are divided up into types: Those that involve breath control, reciting mantra, visualization, etc. The effects obtained by practicing them are based on the individual's preexisting spiritual inclinations. They are not a test. The practice and the experience are personal.

The aspirant should sincerely practice the simpler techniques and will gradually develop the abilities to move to the more complex practices.

The practitioner will find that he or she is more suited to certain types of techniques, in which case more effort should be applied to those.

Background Concepts

Spirituality

Most spiritual seekers accept the existence of god as the creator of the universe, infinite, omnipresent and omnipotent. The question then arises that if god exists everywhere, why do we not perceive him directly in our daily lives? What is the relationship of the individual being with the divine? How can a limited being perceive the infinite? How can I commune directly with the divine?

The answer to these questions can be written in text form so one can read them and intellectually understand them. The truth, however, is not an intellectual concept to be grasped; rather, it is knowledge that has to be intuitively understood and directly experienced. The techniques laid out are for obtaining these experiences.

The section below lays out some concepts to aid in the techniques. They are not designed to contradict any religious or philosophical belief of the reader, but rather as a tool to aid the reader. As stated previously, the techniques stand alone and the experiences will be the same regardless of one's own belief system. (I have tested these techniques on my own students of all different religious persuasions and the results have been the same).

The beginning

Let us assume that in the beginning, prior to the creation of the phenomenal universe, god existed by himself. By definition, then, he is the subject. There is no object, as there is nothing else. No "other," so to speak. No duality. No universe, no time or space, just the unmanifest divinity. Unmanifest is a difficult term to describe as it means not pertaining to name or form in the sense we understand. Thus, prior to creation, god exists in a form that has no material substance; no time or space exists at this point. This cannot be grasped intellectually. This point we will designate as Shiva. From the perspective of god, there is only "I."

This is the zero point.

Creation

The manifest universe we see, with stars and planets, has emerged from a singularity or bindu (literally dot). This manifestation is Shiva with a dynamic aspect termed Shakti (literally "energy"). The two are still aspects of the one and hence there is no duality present. The equivalent would be two sides of one coin. The "I" and the "This" are therefore still one.

At this point, the creator and the creation do not exist separately but are one and the same. A more appropriate term would be "manifestation," as creation implies a creator separate from the creation. The universe we see is nothing more than divine consciousness manifesting itself. A descent has occurred from the single Shiva to the dual -- Shiva and Shakti -- though as stated there is still no duality at this point. If one travels further along this descent then one arrives at the individual. .

The individual

The individual exists with the sense of duality. "I" am separate from "This," with "This" representing the universe around us and also the Divine. The individual is limited by knowledge, form, space and time.

A descending arc of knowledge has occurred from the state of Shiva to the individual, resulting in a limited being existing in a state of duality, separate from the creation. This separation is a perceptual one from the perspective of the individual, who feels the duality and the "ignorance" of the divine.

The purpose of spiritual life is to move on an ascending arc back to the state of Shiva, the zero point.

Ascending the arc

The individual exists within the framework of a limited world: Limited by body, breath, senses, mind, intellect and ego. These will have to be transcended in order to experience the divine.

The Shiva point exists within the individual as the consciousness or soul at the top of the head, in a place yogically termed the Sahasrara (literally, the thousand-petalled Lotus). The Shakti exists in the individual at the base of the spine and is termed Kundalini (or Ki or Chi depending on the philosophical origin).

Ascent to Shiva or the zero point involves merging one's Shakti with the Shiva and experiencing the state of non-duality where there is no "otherness."

Chakras

There are seven main chakras going from the base of the spine to the apex of the cranium. At the base of the spine is the Muladhara chakra, in the lower abdomen is the Svadishthana chakra and at the level of the navel is the Manipura chakra. Above these the individual's level of spiritual development becomes higher. At the level of the heart is the Anahata chakra, the throat is the Visuddha chakra and between the eyes is the Ajna chakra. At this level the individual has transcended duality and time and space. Above this, at the top, is the Sahasrara chakra, which represents the state of Shiva or perfection.

Meditation

Meditation involves practices that require concentration of the mind (Dharana) to make it one-pointed. Once this has occurred, a contemplative state (Dhyana) ensues in which the mind is no longer exerting "effort" to keep itself one-pointed. After this occurs the state of Samadhi, which is a non-dual state in which the knower, known and knowledge merge. It is a state of superconciousness. It is the goal of meditation. As a general rule, meditation involves stilling the mind, as it is a great hindrance on the spiritual path. The mind is made to concentrate on one thing and thus becomes one-pointed. After this the kundalini starts to rise and energy flows more freely through the pranic channels (nada). The higher the kundalini rises, the higher the individual's spiritual state will be. Mere concentration for a period of time, after which one feels relaxed, is not true meditation. One needs to go to a deeper level where the mind is completely still and one experiences what I describe as a state of attunement. As he or she advances, the yogi may feel a buzzing sensation or pressure in the head. These are signs of arousal of the kundalini.

Maya (illusion)

The phenomenal world appears to be separate from us due to Maya, which is the concept of illusion. The illusion is that we exist separate from the creation, with an existence beginning with birth and ending in death, limited egos trapped in limited bodies subject to time and space. The illusion seems very real in our lives. It is created by our senses, mind and ego. Overcoming these is the key to spiritual success. We will use the very attributes that create our ignorance to remove that veil.

Types of Techniques

Techniques using Breath/Prana control

Breath is inextricably linked to life. The moment we are born we start to breath, and when breath ends, life also departs. The breath is linked to a form of divine consciousness termed Prana. This is one of the first phases of the descent of divine consciousness to manifestation. Prana is an energy existing everywhere but also linked with one's breath and one's mind.

Control of the breath and mind are key elements of ascending the arc. Prana moves in channels through the body, termed nada. Controlling the prana allows clearing of the channels and allows the kundalini to ascend to the top. The central channel in the spine is termed sushumna, and connects the kundalini at the bottom with the Shiva at the top. There are various connections along this channel called chakras, as previously described. Each one of these is associated with higher levels of consciousness. Moving one's kundalini along the sushumna to higher and higher levels is part of ascending the arc. Once the kundalini reaches the chakra in the forehead between the eyebrows (termed the Ajna chakra) the individual's state of duality is transcended.

In these techniques we will control our breath by counting it mentally. This has the dual effect of stilling not only our breath but also our mind. Since the mind is constantly wandering from one object of fancy to another, the techniques allow us to use the breath and prana as a means of stilling the mind. The techniques are simple, since the only prerequisite is the ability to count!

Techniques using Mantra

Mantra literally means "instrument of thought." It is a sacred syllable or phrase that can be used to focus the mind. The grossest form of a mantra is at the Vaikhari or verbal stage. This would be at the bottom of the arc. Here duality between the self and the mantra is firmly established. Above this is the mantra repeated as a thought at the level of the mind. At this stage there is still a duality associated with the mantra and it is termed the middle or Madhyama stage.

Above this is the Pashyanti stage ("seeing" level). There is no longer any thought of repeating the mantra, it becomes self-sustaining. Here the mantra and the individual are "merging;" at this point the Shiva component is predominant and there is an indistinct experience of the individual self and phenomenal universe. At this stage duality has effectively ceased. The final stage is Paravik, where the "word" of the mantra exists in an unmanifest and undifferentiated form with no duality at the Shiva level. The individual has effectively become the mantra at the Shiva level. Here one is at the top of the arc.

Techniques using Mudra

Mudra literally means a "seal" or posture, usually denoting a hand position. These positions are universal in yoga practice and help to focus and channel prana. Some are associated with certain chakras. A great exercise to prove the effect of mudra and breath is outlined below.

Sit comfortably either cross-legged on the floor, preferably with a pillow below your buttocks, or sit upright in a chair. Touch the tip of your index finger to the tip of your thumb to create a circle and keep the remaining fingers straight. Place your hands on your thighs, palms up. Close your eyes and breath slowly in a relaxed manner for a minute or two. Observe the pattern of your breathing. Now change the finger position so that the ring finger and the thumb are now opposed and continue breathing. You will notice a definite change in the pattern of the breath. This observation can be practiced using the other mudras shown in the mudras illustrations. Mudras are used to direct the prana to different chakras depending on what the yogi is trying to achieve.

Techniques using the Void

These techniques fall into a more difficult realm of practice and consist of attempting to take oneself into the void, or Sunya. "Void" in this context means a place of no support, i.e., no thoughts, no objective phenomena and no objective existence. It is not, however, a place of non-existence: Since Shiva is the underlying support of the phenomenal universe; it is thus a transcendent state beyond thought.

Once the mind has been stilled by practice of the breath and prana exercises, meditation on the void will be much easier and you will be able to experience the foundational consciousness of Shiva free of any thought constructs (Vikalpas).

Techniques using Visualization and Emotion

These techniques require you to bring the mind under control and visualize certain things such as fire (Kalagni technique). By doing so the mind is focused and becomes still, and the meditative experience proceeds from there.

Certain of the techniques involve using emotion. Emotions are a product of the mind, and you might ask how this can truly lead to a divine state. You have to remember that the underlying consciousness supporting the emotion is the goal. You are using the technique to ascend the arc back to the underlying foundation of the emotion. Emotions are an everyday part of life and some, such as anger, can be very intense. When you are angry, the mind is still and focused, albeit on the anger. This allows you to be taken into a transcendent state if you are able to utilize the stillness of the mind created by the emotion.

List of Techniques

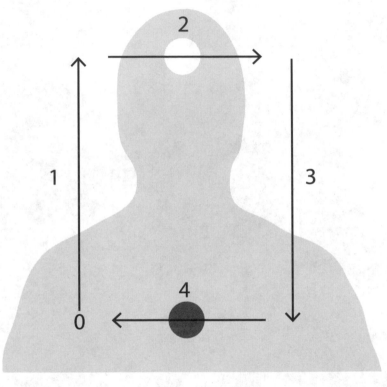

○ Ajna – Essence of All Elements
● Anahata – Air

Technique 1

Technique one (Breath/Mudra)

Sit in a chair or cross-legged, whichever is comfortable. Place your hands in mudra 1 (index finger to thumb -- meditation mudra). The back needs to be straight. This can also be done while lying flat. Close your eyes.

Imagine the breath starting at the level of the heart, in the center, and count an inhalation of four counts: One, one, one, one. The breath should be brought from the heart area to the middle of the forehead as you count. Hold the breath here, suspended, and concentrate your mind at this point. Count the suspension, again as a four count: Two, two, two, two. Exhale the breath back down to the heart area again in a four count: Three, three, three, three.

Suspend the breath here, again for a four count: Four, four, four, four.

Then relax for a split second and count zero before resuming the count and starting the cycle again.

Here, "one" represents inhalation, "two" suspension after inhalation, "three" is exhalation and "four" is suspension after exhalation. "Zero" represents a totally static state prior to the commencement of any breath.

Do this for several minutes until it is comfortable. It is important to count the different phases of the breath, as this keeps your mind concentrated. Then start going to a three count on the inhalation, suspension, etc. for a few minutes, then a two count for a few minutes and finally a one count.

At this point your breath and mind will be fairly still. Now try and extend out the suspension point to hold them longer. This should be done comfortably and without straining the body. The mind must remain at the Ajna chakra and the heart chakra during the suspension. Try not to let it wander. At this point one can drop the counting during the suspension.

This technique is for developing the central channel and allowing the kundalini to rise. After practice, you may feel the effects of the kundalini rising as a pressure sensation in the head, or as a feeling of "buzzing" or vibration in the head or ears. Some people perceive light in the Ajna chakra.

The suspension point is where the mind, breath and prana are completely still. If you develop these points you start to experience a point of total stillness. Ordinarily you might expect that if the breath and mind are completely stilled, you would experience a nihilistic state of non-existence. This, however, does not occur. Instead, in the stillness you experience the consciousness in its pure form, the state of Shiva.

This technique is very simple to practice and allows the mind to become still relatively quickly. I have used this technique as the starting point for other techniques that are more difficult as it allows one to enter them with the mind already free of thought constructs.

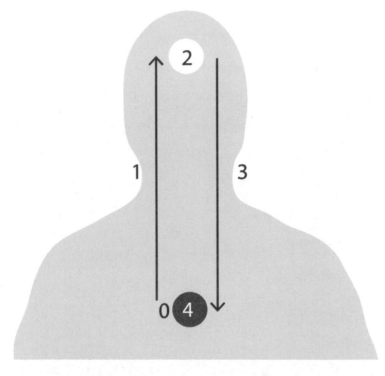

○ Ajna – Essence of All Elements

● Anahata – Air

Technique 2

Technique two (Breath)

This techniques involves observation of the breath in a relaxed state.

Observe that the breath starts at the level of the heart and terminates at the level of the mouth or nose. There is a point, albeit brief, of natural suspension between the ingoing and outgoing breath at these levels. Quiet observation of these still points will lead to a Shiva state. Again, you can passively count the breath in its different stages as in technique one.

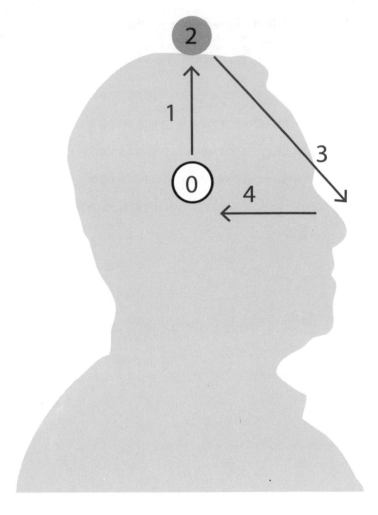

● Sahasrara – Beyond Elements
○ Ajna – Essence of All Elements

Technique 3

Technique three (Breath)

Sit in meditative posture with meditation mudra and eyes closed.

Imagine the breath starting at a point in the middle of the head at a level of the ear canals (pineal gland). Start inhaling, counting one, one, one, one. The inhalation is upward to the top of the skull. Suspend the breath here for a four count (two, two, two, two). Exhale in a line to the tip of the nose, again with a four count. Suspend the breath here for a four count. The zero point from which the cycle starts again is the point inside the middle of the head at the level of the ear canals. As in technique one, gradually decrease the counts over several minutes to a three count, then two and then one. After this try and maintain the suspension points for longer periods. You will be pervaded by a feeling of stillness and tranquility.

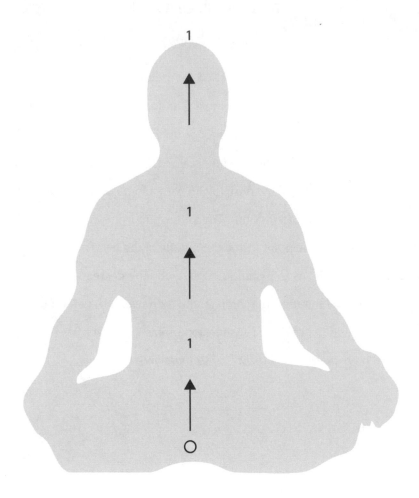

Muladhara – Earth

Technique 4

Technique four (Breath)

Starting at the base of the spine in the Muladhara chakra (Mula -- base, Adhara -- support), count an inhalation of one, one, one, taking the breath to the level of the apex of the head with the final count. Suspend the breath here for a few seconds, as long as feels comfortable, and then exhale. Repeat the exercise, taking the breath from the base chakra to the top of the head (apex of the cranium) in a count of three during the inhalation.

The kundalini will rise and you will be dissolved in the Shiva state.

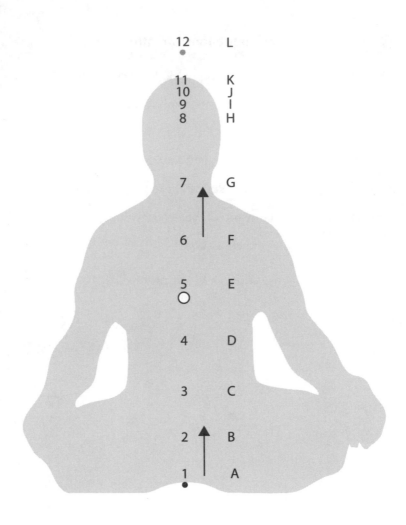

12 Sahasrara

5 Ajna

Technique 5

Technique five (Breath/visualization)

Starting at the base of the spine, count from 1 through 12, all the way up to the apex of the cranium. The five count should be at the heart chakra, the eight count at the Ajna chakra and the remaining counts to the top of the head. This can be done in one inhalation. The kundalini in this exercise is rising through the successive chakras to the top. There are seven main chakras and five minor ones. Alternatively, you may use letters such as A, B, C, etc. During this and the last technique the kundalini must be visualized moving up the spine to the top.

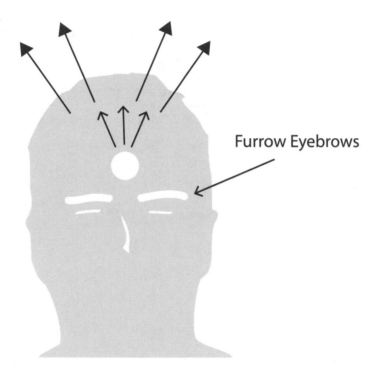

Furrow Eyebrows

Technique 6

Technique six

Concentrate pranic energy in the Ajna chakra using any of the above techniques. Perform bhruksepa, which means to furrow the eyebrows. This leads to the prana being converted into Shakti-consciousness. Imagine it going up to and out of the apex of the cranium. You will have an experience of omnipresence. This is a harder technique and requires you to have already developed one-pointedness of mind.

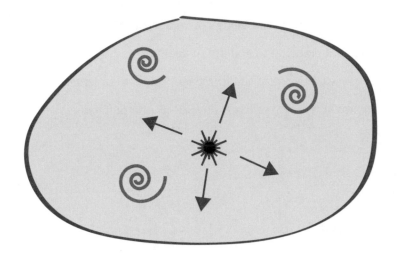

Sound ⟶ Space
Contemplate sound of
Big Bang and its relationship
to product of space.

Technique 7

Technique seven (Breath/visualization)

This technique involves trying to get to the origin of the senses.

In yogic science the five senses, or tanmatras, are sound, touch, form, taste and fragrance. Each of these has a corresponding element. From sound comes space, from touch comes air, from form comes fire, from taste comes water and from fragrance comes earth. An example of how to understand these relationships is to consider that the Big Bang (sound) preceded the formation of the space of the universe. The technique involves meditating on the abstract quality of sound, form, etc. and imagining them as a void. This is a difficult technique to master.

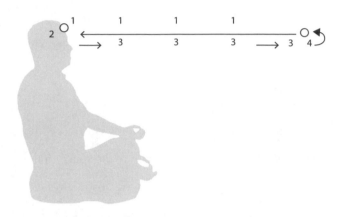

Gradually decelerate count.

Maintain suspension
at zero point.

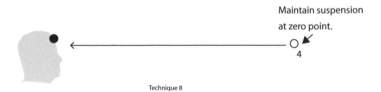

Technique 8

Technique eight (Breath/visualization/void)

Start with technique one to make the mind one-pointed. Then, gazing into an open space such as the sky, imagine the zero point in the sky. Count the inhalation from the zero point to the center of your forehead (Ajna chakra). As in technique one, this is a four count. Suspend here for a four count and exhale back to the external zero point, again doing a suspension there. Gradually decelerate the counts from a four count down to a one count as in technique one. Try and suspend your mind at the external zero point. You will be merged in the void.

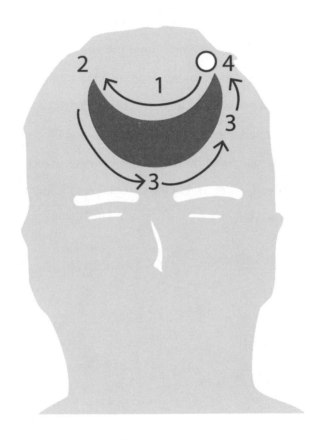

Technique 9

Technique nine (Chakra/breath/visualization)

Imagine a crescent moon in your forehead with the larger curve downward and the smaller curve facing upward. Start at the left top of the smaller curve and count a four count of inhalation, taking yourself along the lesser curve to the right side of it. Suspend at that point for a four count and then exhale along the larger curve from the right side to the left, doing a four count. Suspend at the left side for a four count and start the sequence again with zero. Gradually reduce the count as in technique one until you are at a one count. This technique brings you into the Ajna chakra

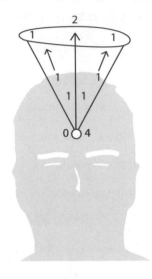

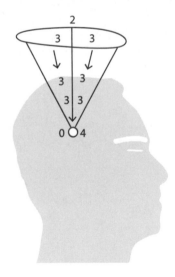

Technique10

Technique ten (Breath/visualization)

Start with the zero point at the pineal gland and imagine a funnel expanding from this point to outside the top of your head. Start your four count inhalation, expanding from the pineal through the funnel and outside the top of your head. Suspend for a four count outside the head and exhale back to the pineal gland. Suspend the breath here for a four count and start again with zero. Gradually decrease the counts to a one count. Expand the suspension points outside the head and at the pineal gland.

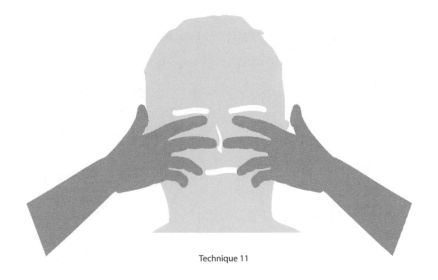

Technique 11

Technique eleven (Mudra)

The mudra used for this technique is termed trikabanda. It involves cutting off all external senses so that the seeker is left with the consciousness alone. Use both hands block the eyes with the index fingers, the nose with the middle fingers, the ears with the thumbs and place the ring and little fingers on the mouth.

The yogi will hear the hum of the inner self and will gradually discern a bright light in the Ajna chakra region. If you concentrate on this it will be dissolved, and the Shiva state ensues.

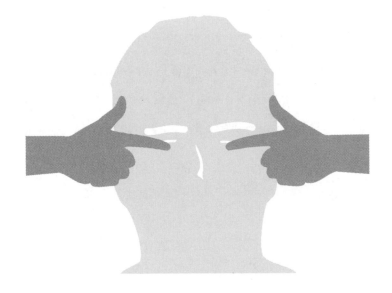

Technique 12

Technique twelve (Mudra)

Similar to the last technique except the yogi only places his or her index finger over the eyes. This will cause the appearance of certain visual aura and lights. Focus on one of these lights and concentrate on the region at the top of the head or in the heart chakra. This will make the mind one-pointed and, with practice, thought-free.

○ Ajna
● Visudha

0 ○ 4
        ↑
      1

      3
   1 ↑

      3
   1 ↑

   1

   ●2

Technique 13

Technique thirteen (Concentration)

This technique is one of "listening" to the vibration of the kundalini within yourself.

After a period of meditation and some degree of kundalini arousal, you will start to hear a kind of buzzing or vibration that occurs during meditation. This will gradually become more frequent until it occurs every time you meditate. With time this will occur spontaneously, even when you are not meditating. It is perceived at different places, such as the Ajna chakra, heart chakra or at the level of the ear. It has been my experience that with practice one can use it to aid in very intense meditation, as the vibration increases in intensity and can be concentrated at the chakra that the yogi wishes. The vibration itself is termed Anahata Nada, or unstruck sound. It is sound that exists in the universe in an as-yet un-manifest state. It is said to arise from the heart or Anahata chakra. The effect is often felt after the yogi has been initiated by an enlightened guru. This is termed Shaktipat diksha and is the direct transmission of spiritual knowledge and energy from the guru to the student. It has the effect of initiating the kundalini from an essentially dormant state to an aroused state. Spiritual progress accelerates after such an occurrence. It is possible to perceive this sound even if you have not been initiated, but more effort is required. Personally, I would have this experience during concentrated meditation prior to being initiated.

Start with the zero point at the pineal gland and count the inhalation to the throat area. Then suspend the breath here and exhale to the pineal gland again. Suspend here. As per technique one, the breath can be gradually reduced to a one count for the inhalation, exhalation and suspension points. Concentration should be focused on the zero point. Use the mudra with the middle finger touching the thumb.

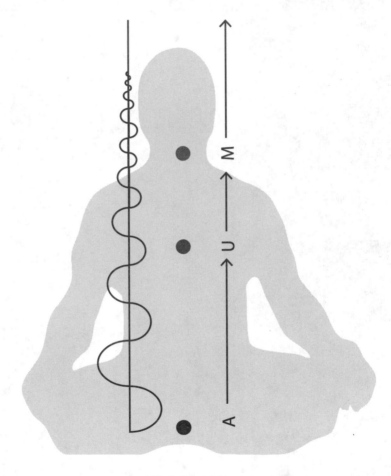

Technique 14

Technique fourteen (Om mantra)

This technique uses the Om mantra, which is designated as the primordial sound. That does not mean that the universe is vibrating with the Om sound made by the yogi. Rather it implies that the Om sound is the sound of creation at the descending portion of the arc. We are to use the mantra to ascend back to the Shiva point and experience the Om at the Shiva level. The mantra consists of four syllables. Three are pronounced and the last syllable is not. The A, U and M parts of the mantra are pronounced either verbally or, better still, mentally. The mantra should be practiced with a fourth syllable that is not pronounced, but is where the yogi effectively tails off the mantra. The beginning of the Om should start at the level of the abdomen and the M portion should end at the level of the mouth. Imagine the Om vibrating on a fine thread that starts at your abdomen and goes out the top of your head. The Om should be seen as vibrating the string. The non-pronounced Om is from the mouth to the top of the head, where you visualize the vibration of the string becoming finer and finer. The pronounced Om can be done with an inhalation, while during exhalation you visualize the Om in the fourth phase continuing up ever finer. The three syllables of the Om represent the waking, dreaming and deep sleep states of the individual, while the fourth syllable represents the state beyond this, termed Turiya. The Turiya state is like the witnessing consciousness of the other three states, the underlying substratum for them. It is often understood by phrases such as "the ear of the ear" or "the eye of the eye." These phrases have to be intuitively understood by prolonged and deep meditation.

Thus practicing the Om, you will gradually attain the Shiva state.

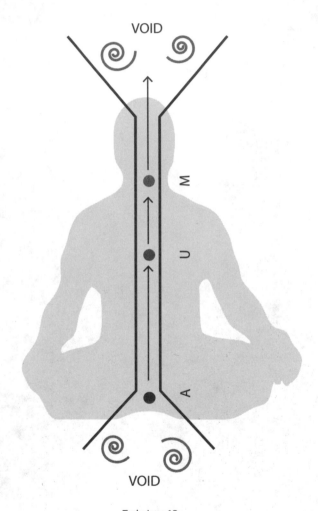

Technique 15

Technique fifteen (Mantra/void)

Practice technique fourteen using the Om mantra. Contemplate the void at the beginning and end of the mantra. To do this you may imagine the Om starting at the level of the abdomen, below which is a vast and infinite void. The Om is then practiced as described in fourteen and ends at the top of the head, again going into an infinite void. The concept of sunya or void has been described in the Types of Techniques section of the book. Again, it is a state of no support. That is to say, no thought constructs of the mind. This technique is used with the meditation mudra.

Techniques sixteen to twenty
(Mantra/mudra/breath/chakras)

The five elements (air, fire, water, earth and space) are also related to the different phases of the breath and to different chakras in the body.

Thus inhalation is associated with air and the heart (Anahata) chakra. Suspension after inhalation is associated with fire and the Manipura chakra. Exhalation is associated with water and the Svadishthana chakra. Suspension after exhalation is associated with earth and the Muladhara chakra. The zero point at the beginning and end of each breath cycle is associated with space and the Visuddha chakra. Each chakra has a seed sound, or Beej mantra, which will be used when contemplating the respective chakra. Each chakra also has its own mudra. Remember when doing the breath counting to always include the zero point. Try and "vibrate" the chakra with the respective beej mantra.

The following techniques are for concentrating on the individual chakras.

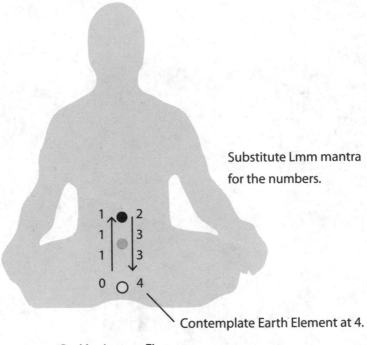

Substitute Lmm mantra for the numbers.

1 ● 2
1 ● 3
1   3
0 ○ 4

Contemplate Earth Element at 4.

● Manipura – Fire
● Svadhishthana – Water
○ Muladhara – Earth

Technique 16

Sixteen

Concentrate on the Muladhara chakra at the base of the spine in the perineal region. The beej mantra is Lmm. The tip of the ring finger touches the tip of the thumb to form a circle.

Concentrate on the earth element during the suspension after exhalation phase of the breath. Count the breath from the base chakra to the mid-abdomen at the level of the Svadisthana or Manipura chakras. The inhalation will go from the base to the abdomen, suspend, then exhale back down to the base chakra and suspend. Your concentration point will be at the base chakra during this suspension, with contemplation of the earth element. Earth in this case does not signify the planet Earth, but rather elemental earth. As you perform inhalation and exhalation, recite the Lmm mantra. Instead of using the numbers for counting, use the Lmm. Again, as with technique one there is a gradual decreasing count. On arousal of this chakra you may perceive a feeling of lightness or you may feel the vibration of nada.

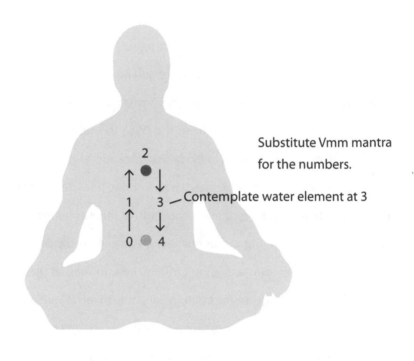

Substitute Vmm mantra for the numbers.

Contemplate water element at 3

● Anahata – Air
● Svadhishthana – Water

Technique 17

Seventeen

Concentrate on the Svadishthana chakra in the lower abdomen. The beej mantra is Vmm. The tip of the little finger and the thumb are touching.

Concentrate on the water element during the exhalation phase of the breath. Count the breath from mid-abdomen at the level of the Svadisthana up to the heart chakra. The inhalation will go from the mid-abdomen, suspend at heart, then exhale back down to the mid-abdomen and suspend. Your concentration point will be at the mid-abdomen during exhalation, with contemplation of the water element. As you perform inhalation and exhalation, recite the Vmm mantra. Instead of using the numbers for counting, use the Vmm. Again, as with technique one there is a gradual decreasing count. This chakra affects apana, one of the types of pranic energy, and practice allows you to free yourself from greed, anger and jealousy.

Substitute Rmm mantra for the numbers.

2 — Contemplate fire element at 2

1 ↑ 2 ● ↓ 3

0 ○ 4

● Manipura – Fire

○ Muladhara – Earth

Technique 18

Eighteen

Concentrate on the Manipura chakra in the mid-abdomen. The beej mantra is Rmm. Place the tip of the ring finger at the base of the thumb and place the thumb across it.

Concentrate on the fire element in the suspension phase after inhalation. Again, the breath can be counted as in the above techniques using the Rmm as the count instead of numbers. Take the breath from the base chakra to the abdomen area for the counts. The concentration point is the suspension point after inhalation, which should be at the level of this chakra. This chakra generates heat and destroys the ego. This chakra allows the yogi to engage in astral travel, although you should obtain instruction in this from your teacher or guru.

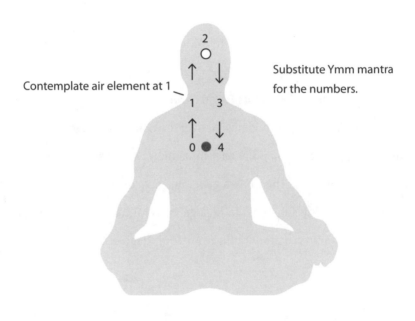

Contemplate air element at 1

Substitute Ymm mantra for the numbers.

○ Ajna – Essence of All Elements
● Anahata – Air

Technique 19

Nineteen

Concentrate on the heart (Anahata) chakra with the beej mantra of Ymm. Place the index finger at the base of the thumb and cross the thumb over the top of it.

Concentrate on the air element in the inhalation phase of the cycle. Take the breath from the heart chakra up to the Ajna chakra. This center is associated with spirituality. The anahata (or unstruck sound) is said to originate in this chakra. The yogi whose consciousness is centered in this chakra obtains intuitive knowledge of Siddhis (supernatural powers). Pursuing these is a hindrance in the pursuit of truth and care must be taken to control the ego.

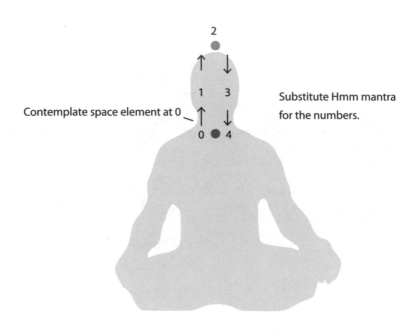

Contemplate space element at 0

Substitute Hmm mantra for the numbers.

● Sahasrara – Beyond Elements
● Vishuddha – Space

Technique 20

Twenty

Concentrating on the throat chakra, fold the middle finger onto the palm with the thumb across it. The beej mantra is Hmm. The breath can be taken between the throat chakra and either up to the Ajna chakra or down to the Anahata chakra. The zero point is at the level of the throat chakra. Concentrate on the space element at the level of the throat at the zero point in the breath cycle.

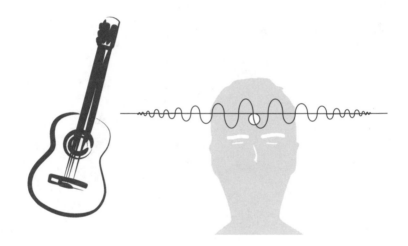

Technique 21

Twenty-one (Concentration/music)

This technique involves listening to the note of a stringed instrument. Concentrate on the Ajna chakra and pluck the string to obtain a note. Let all your concentration focus on the note and the sound. The note should be visualized as coming from the void and being dissolved back into it. You are ascending the arc from the gross sound to the more subtle elements of sound. The nature of sound will be revealed to you.

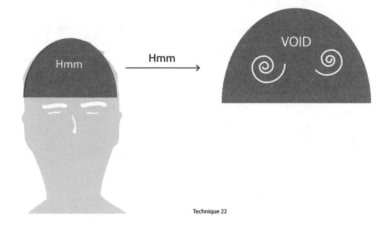

Technique 22

Twenty-two (Void/mantra)

Use the mudra of thumb to index fingertip and the mantra Hmm.
Concentrate on the mantra in the region above the eyebrows to the tip
of the head. Visualize this area as a vast void into which the mantra
is going. Contemplating this leads to merging into the void.

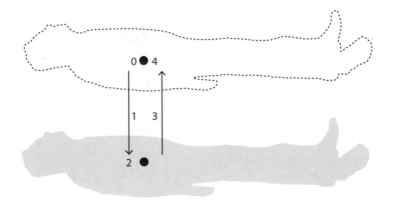

● Manipura – Fire

Technique 23

Twenty-three (Concentration/astral travel)

The next techniques are for astral travel (see technique 18).

I recommend learning these from an experienced teacher or guru, but I have placed them here for the reader to experience.

This technique is best done lying flat on your back. Using the mudra as in technique 18 and concentrating in the mid-abdomen, make your mind still using technique one. Then contemplate rising out of your body above it. Keep the zero point outside and above your body and inhale towards the mid-abdomen. Suspend your breath here and exhale back to the zero point. As you exhale visualize yourself going out with the breath. Again as in technique one, the yogi should start with a four count on all the phases and gradually decrease them. If the technique is done correctly, you will initially feel a sensation of lightness. Then you will see yourself above your body. This is not your imagination: The feeling is as real as if you were completely awake and having the same experience. You can then travel at will.

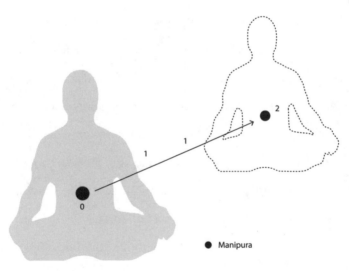

● Manipura

Technique 24

Twenty-four (Concentration/astral travel)

This is a different astral travel technique. Using the mudra as above, concentrate on the mid-abdomen and make your mind still using technique one. Then contemplate the place you wish to travel to. The zero point is in your mid-abdomen; take your inhalation towards the place you wish to travel to. The key is to do the suspension after the inhalation at the new place. The yogi "travels" during the inhalation phase and "appears" during the suspension phase. The length of the distance is irrelevant.

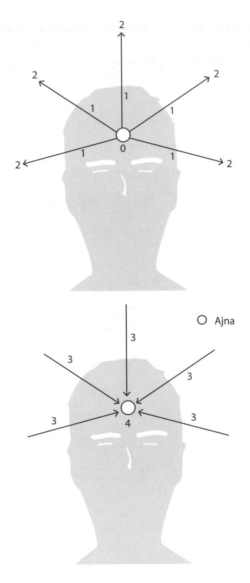

Technique 25

Twenty-five (Breath/concentration/void)

Use the mudra of index finger tip to thumb tip. Concentrate on the Ajna chakra and still the mind as in technique one. Then start with the Ajna chakra as the zero point and start the inhalation count, imagining it going out from your Ajna chakra in all directions, encompassing vast space. Suspend the breath in the vast space and exhale back to the Ajna chakra. Begin again at the zero point. By contemplating such, you are merged into the void.

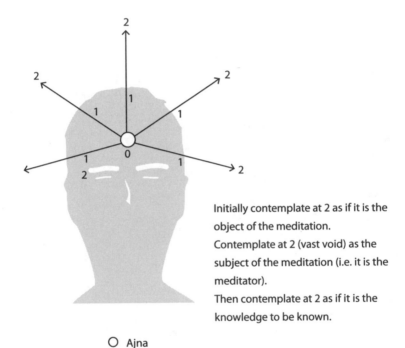

Initially contemplate at 2 as if it is the object of the meditation.

Contemplate at 2 (vast void) as the subject of the meditation (i.e. it is the meditator).

Then contemplate at 2 as if it is the knowledge to be known.

O Ajna

Technique 26

Twenty-six (Concentration/void)

Perform the above technique and then try to think of the void as the object of your one-pointed thought. Contemplate it as if it is the subject and finally, as if the void is the knowledge itself. This is a difficult technique of merging the knower, known and knowledge into the void. A state of Shiva will arise.

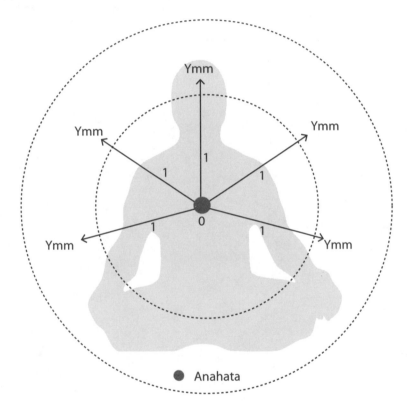

Ymm

Ymm

Ymm

Ymm

Ymm

Ymm

1

1

1

1

1

1

0

● Anahata

Technique 27

Twenty-seven (Concentration/void)

Contemplate any chakra with the respective mudra (see techniques 16-20).

Visualize the chakra as the vast space of the universe within yourself. Use the breath technique outlined in technique one. The space expands within you as you concentrate on the beej mantra and its respective chakra. The chakra expands as you inhale. Your thoughts are dissolved in the vast void and you enter the state of Shiva.

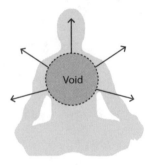

● Anahata

Technique 28

Twenty-eight (Concentration/void)

Similar to the above, imagine your body within, organs, blood, inside the skull, etc., as nonexistent and pervaded by space. This practice will gradually break your attachment to and identification with the body.

Starts at right big toe

Technique 29

Twenty-nine (Visualization/kalagni -- fire)

This technique is termed kalagni. Visualize yourself being consumed by fire, beginning at the right big toe and gradually moving up and destroying the whole body. This practice allows you to break your association with the physical body. What is left after the body is consumed is your essential nature. You are merged with your individual consciousness.

Starts at right big toe

Technique 30

Thirty (Kalagni)

Similar to above, imagine that the fire continues and dissolves everything around you. It gradually expands to dissolve the whole universe. That which remains after the burning of the phenomenal universe is Shiva. You are merged in the total consciousness.

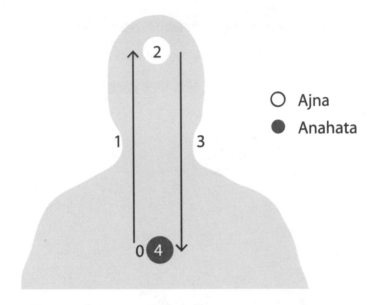

Dissolving elements into their constituent forms.

0 Space into Sound

1 Air into Touch

2 Fire into Form

3 Water into Taste

4 Earth into Smell

Technique 31

Thirty-one (Breath/visualization)

The next technique is moderately difficult as it presupposes some degree of intuitive knowledge of the subject.

As stated in (7), the five senses or tanmatras are sound, touch, form, taste and fragrance. Each of these has a corresponding element. From sound comes space, from touch comes air, from form comes fire, from taste comes water and from fragrance comes earth. We have seen that each of these has a respective chakra and phase of the breath cycle.

We will start by concentrating on the heart chakra to the Ajna chakra. As in technique one, begin by breathing through the different phases of inhalation, suspension, etc.

Then dissolve space into sound at the zero point. Air is dissolved into touch at the inhalation phase, followed by form dissolved into fire at the suspension phase. In exhalation water is dissolved into taste and in the last suspension earth is dissolved into smell. This technique involves breaking down the universe into its gross form and tracing it back to its subtler form, ascending the arc, if you will. The point arises above the level of thought where these constituent elements exist in a non-dual undifferentiated form. This is your goal. This cannot be adequately explained in words and requires intuitive understanding.

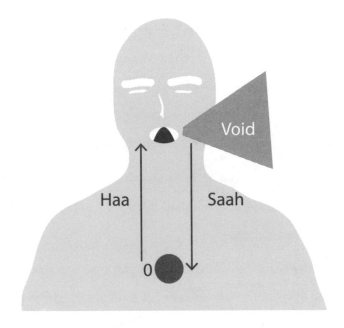

● Dissolve space into sound at Anahata Chakra

Technique 32

Thirty-two (Breath/chakra)

This technique allows you to control your dreams. Place the index finger at the base of the thumb and cross the thumb over the top of it. Start the zero point at the heart chakra. Place the tongue at the top of the palate with the mouth open and inhale, making a subtle haa sound. The suspension point is at the opening of the mouth, beyond which you should visualize a void. Exhale with a subtle saah sound. Dissolve the elements of space and sound in the heart chakra. If you sleep while doing this practice you will have control of your dreams.

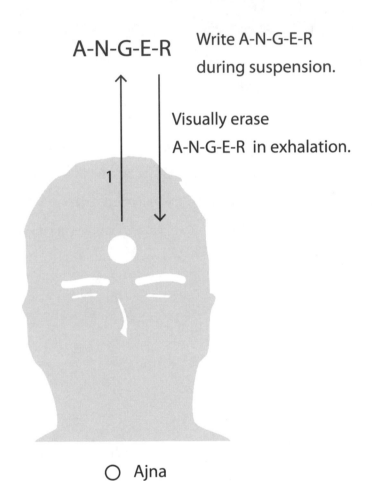

A-N-G-E-R   Write A-N-G-E-R
during suspension.

Visually erase
A-N-G-E-R in exhalation.

1

○ Ajna

Technique 33

Thirty-three (Visualization)

This technique allows you to remove emotions that may hinder your progress.

Sit with index fingertip to thumb and concentrate on the area above the forehead. Breathe from the Ajna chakra to the top of the head. At the first suspension point after inhalation, visually write the quality that you wish to dissolve. For instance, mentally write A-N-G-E-R in the crown area of your head during the suspension and then wipe it off mentally during exhalation. The characteristic will diminish in you.

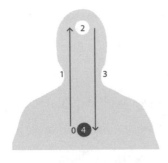

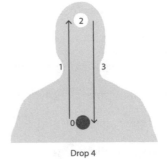

Drop 4

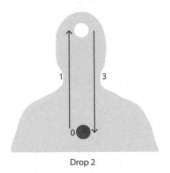

Drop 2

Drop 1

Merge in breath and out breath at zero.

○ Ajna
● Anahata

Technique 34

Thirty-four (Breath/visualization)

The zero point in the breathing cycles that we have been practicing represent the state of Shiva. This is a state of spirit with no matter. We live in a universe where matter and spirit exist together in varying amounts, including within ourselves. In this technique, contemplate the zero point as being devoid of movement, flow, heat, taste, thought, etc.

Practice this exercise by breathing as in technique one. The heart or Ajna chakra can be used. Then drop the suspension after exhalation. You are now inhaling, suspending and going to the zero point. Then drop the suspension after inhalation and breathe in from zero and out to zero. Finally, drop the inhalation and be at zero. This zero must be perceived as the Shiva point.

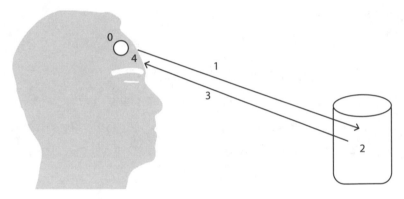

Technique 35

Thirty-five (Void)

Stare into the space in a jar. Start with the zero point at Ajna chakra and count the inhalation towards the jar. This phase is a slower count than normal. The suspension point occurs within the jar. Feel your consciousness unfold into the jar. Exhale back to the Ajna chakra. Once you have become comfortable with this, imagine the jar as being totally void of anything. You are then absorbed into the void.

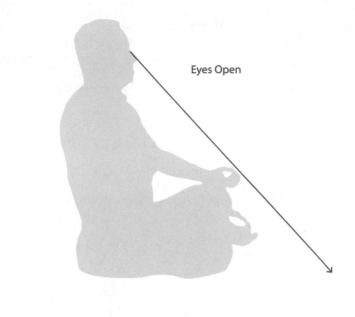

Eyes Open

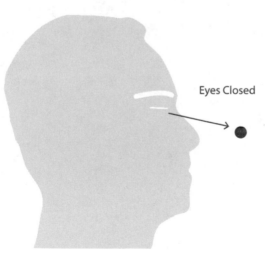

Eyes Closed

Technique 36

Thirty-six (Void)

Stare into empty space or at the ground several feet in front of you. Keep your concentration at the tip of your nose as you are staring. Concentrate your gaze for several minutes and then close your eyes and focus the concentration 1 inch above the nose tip. You will be engulfed in a red aura, which is the nature of void.

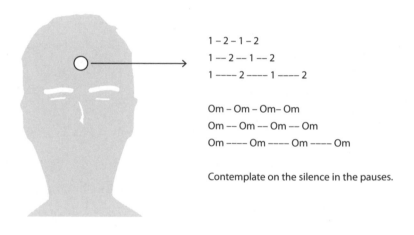

1 – 2 – 1 – 2
1 –– 2 –– 1 –– 2
1 ––– 2 ––– 1 ––– 2

Om – Om – Om– Om
Om –– Om –– Om –– Om
Om ––– Om ––– Om ––– Om

Contemplate on the silence in the pauses.

O Ajna

Technique 37

Thirty-seven (Contemplation)

This technique can be practiced many ways. The goal is to allow yourself to linger on the gap between two thoughts. The gap is the space where the foundational consciousness that allows us to think the thoughts exists. If there is no thought then we are merged into our own innate state.

Touch the tip of the index finger to thumb and concentrate your thoughts at the Ajna chakra. Most simply, you can think of repeating the number one followed by the number two. Keep repeating 1, 2, 1, 2, etc. and then pause between them. No other thought must be allowed to enter. You must also not have any expectation of an experience, as the state between the thoughts is actually the subject, the object and the knowledge that you are seeking. You should practice this so that no new thought appears during the silence. If you are able to maintain this, then the Shiva state will appear. You can also achieve this by repeating Om and concentrating on the gap between the Om. The same principle applies to listening to music where one is absorbed in the music. It is, however, the gap between the notes that leads to the feeling of bliss and elation. In the case of music one is experiencing the "ear of the ear."

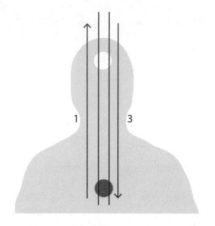 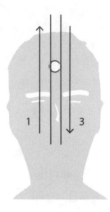

O Ajna
● Anahata

Technique 38

Thirty-eight (Breath/prana)

Touch the tip of the index finger to the thumb. Contemplate the breath at the level above the eyebrows. The breath coming in and out goes through a channel in the spine coming out the top of your head. As you breathe in from the level of the heart chakra to the crown area, the prana moves up, as you exhale, it moves down from above the head to the crown area. The incoming breath and outgoing breath are merged in this area. Gradually merge the breaths and cease all movement. Contemplate this state.

Contemplate bliss as pervading each phase of breath and each element.

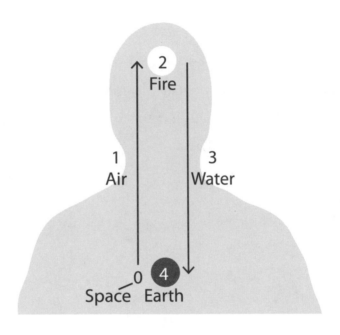

O   Ajna
●   Anahata

Technique 39

Thirty-nine (Contemplation/breath)

In this technique, contemplate the nature of bliss. This should not be thought of as an emotion such as joy, but rather as the eternal underlying essence of existence. The breath should be practiced as in technique one where each stage, i.e., inhalation, suspension, etc. are all pervaded by this bliss. Then you can move on to perceiving each element of the breath cycle as pervaded by bliss. That is, during inhalation the air, in suspension the fire, in exhalation the water and in suspension the earth, are all pervaded by this bliss, as well as at the zero point, which is space.

○ Ajna

Technique 40

Forty (Experiences)

During a beautiful experience such as a sunset, musical piece, the birth of a child, etc., you will experience a state of bliss where the mind is stilled and thought-free as it is overcome by the joy. In this state you can experience the state of Shiva as the subject (the yogi), the object of joy and the experience of joy are all merged. Holding onto these experiences of bliss gives insight into what the Shiva state should be. If you concentrate on the inhalation and suspension after inhalation during the episode then you will have a heightened state of bliss.

O Ajna

Technique 41

Forty-one (Experience)

Similar to the above experiences except it includes even simpler life events such as tasting a delicious meal or meeting an old friend, etc. The experience of these is less intense and shorter than the experience in (40), but if you are aware you can use them to take yourself to the Shiva state. Now if you think back on such an event you can often bring the same state forward and relive the experience. The bliss felt during these occurs because the mind is still. The bliss is not "coming" from anywhere but is your underlying essential nature, which is normally filtered out by thoughts and the mind.

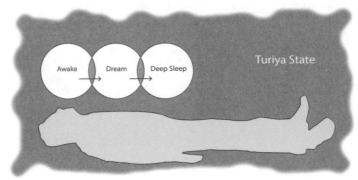

Turiya is the foundational conciousness for the three other states.

Technique 42

Forty-two (Turiya state)

The individual exists in the world in three states: The waking state, where he or she has "I"ness and perception of the external world, the dream state, where the "I"ness is present but the external world no longer exists, and the deep sleep state, where the "I"ness does not exist but the individual has "knowledge" that the state has occurred. All three of these are possible because of an underlying state of consciousness called the Turiya state. This state can be experienced at the transition points between the other states. If you remain aware as you are falling asleep, you will experience the Turiya state just prior to going into the dream state of sleep. The Turiya state is the underlying foundational consciousness that allows the other three states to exist. This relationship is symbolized by the Om sign. See also (50).

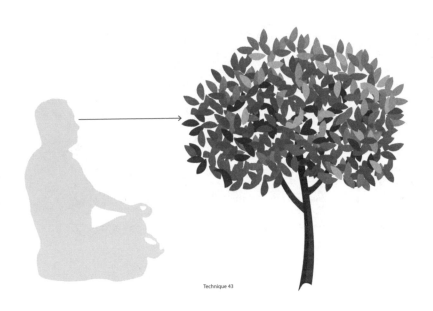

Technique 43

Forty-three (Concentration)

In this technique, gaze at patterns of different colors, textures or shades. An example would be looking at sunlight streaming into a room or gazing at leaves on a tree being blown by the wind. Gaze at the pattern and then withdraw your concentration from it. By contemplating the area of transition you are able to transcend your limited consciousness. This requires a yogi practiced in one-pointed contemplation and would seem relatively hard to most people.

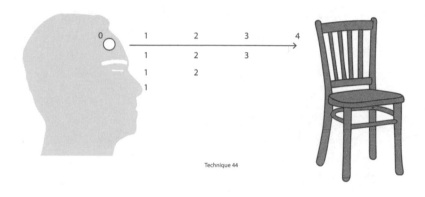

Technique 44

Forty-four (Concentration/visualization)

Practice drawing the mind inward. Gaze fixedly at an external object while drawing your senses inward. This can be done by creating an imaginary line between the object and Ajna chakra. Count from the object 4, 3, 2,1, 0, where the 4 is at the object and 0 is at the Ajna chakra. The count then goes 3, 2,1,0 and 2,1, 0, etc. until you are at the Ajna chakra. The gaze must be maintained on the object during the exercise. This technique allows you to keep the mind focused internally despite having the eyes open.

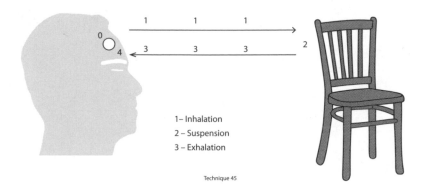

1 – Inhalation
2 – Suspension
3 – Exhalation

Technique 45

Forty-five

This is similar to (44). Gaze at the object and use your Ajna chakra as the zero point. Inhale toward the object, suspend there and exhale back to the Ajna chakra. The point of concentration is the zero point. This can start with a four count on the inhalation, suspension, etc. and gradually reduce to a one count. You perceive that the essence of the object is no different to yourself.

Alternately, you can keep the Ajna chakra as the zero point and do the inhalation, suspension, etc. internally while gazing at the object.

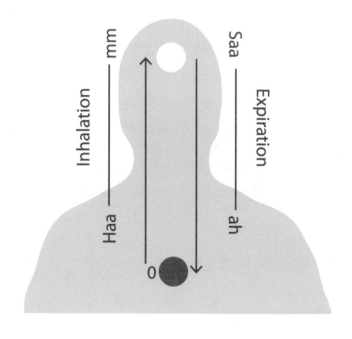

○ Ajna

● Anahata

Technique 46

Forty-six (Mantra)

The Ham-sah mantra is related to breath. The haam portion is performed at inhalation with the mm portion as the suspension and the sahh as the exhalation. This can be done between two chakra, such as the heart and Ajna chakras. The mantra is almost the natural sound made by the breath. Inhale from the heart chakra to the Ajna chakra with the sound haa, then suspend the breath at the Ajna chakra with the mmm portion. Exhale back down to the heart chakra with the sah. The mantra should be recited internally. Since it coincides with the breath it allows the yogi to maintain a spiritual practice virtually all the time.

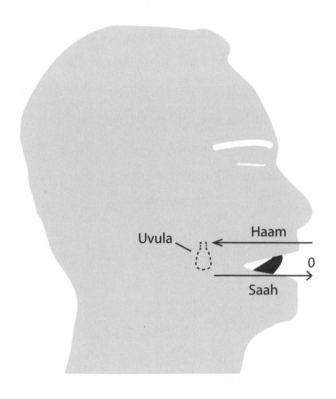

Uvula

Haam

0

Saah

Technique 47

Forty-seven (Mudra)

This is khechari mudra. Open the mouth and place the tongue at the top of the palate. Breathe in and out with the sound haa. This can be done mentally. The zero point is several inches outside the mouth and the inhalation with haa is done to the uvula. Suspend at this point and exhale to the point outside the mouth. This mudra uses the Hamsah mantra. The Haa portion builds up the kundalini flow in the sushumna channel.

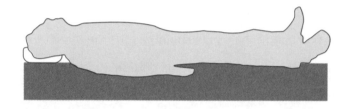

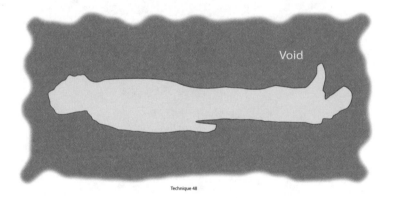

Void

Technique 48

Forty-eight (Concentration)

While lying on a bed or soft sofa, imagine that there is no support for your body. As you breathe, there should be less concentration on the inhalation component and more on the suspension points.

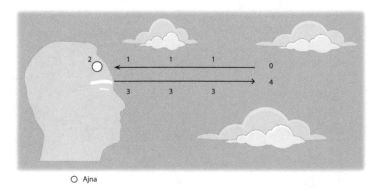

O Ajna

Technique 49

Forty-nine (Void)

Gaze at the open sky. The sky should be the zero point, and the inhalation is to the Ajna chakra. As before, suspend and then exhale back out to the sky and suspend there. Start with a four count and gradually decrease the count to one. Then suspend the zero point longer. You will be merged into the void. During this exercise, as you are gazing at the sky and the mind starts to become one-pointed, it is possible to see the prana moving as very fine swirly lines in the sky.

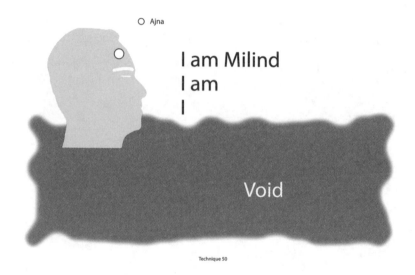

O Ajna

I am Milind
I am
I

Void

Technique 50

Fifty (Turiya state)

This is the state of foundational consciousness and can be passively experienced as in (42) at the transition from the waking to the sleep state.

It can also be experienced by contemplating yourself. Thus contemplate "I AM MILIND," then "I AM," then "I" and finally nothing. This should be practiced at the Ajna chakra, with the index finger tip to the thumb. After the final "I," do not try and think of anything or expect to experience anything, as it is a transcendental state that is beyond the concept of thought and experience. This requires intuitive understanding.

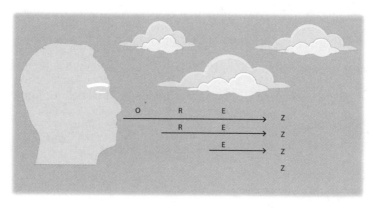

Technique 51

Fifty-one (Void)

This technique is similar to (8). Gaze at the expanse of the sky. Spell out the word ZERO with the O at the mouth and the Z faraway in the sky. Then delete the O and contemplate Z-E-R. Then contemplate Z-E-, and then Z (far away in the sky) and then nothing. Again, do not envisage any expectation of an experience, as you will be in the void, which is free of thought constructs and experiences.

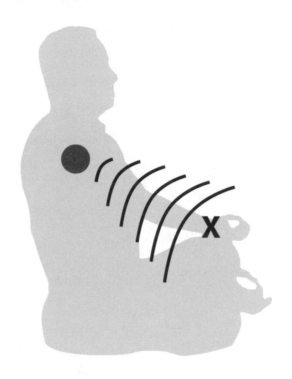

● Anahata – Air

Technique 52

Fifty-two (Sensation)

Pinch yourself or poke yourself with a sharp object. You will feel pain at that spot. By concentrating at that spot the mind becomes one-pointed.

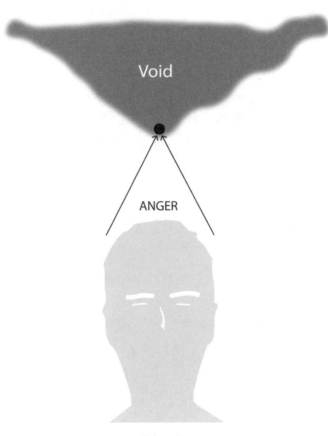

Void

ANGER

Technique 53

Fifty-three (Emotion)

When one has an intense emotion such as anger, the mind becomes one-pointed. It is focused on the anger. If you neither accept nor reject the anger, the thought processes cease and you experience the underlying principle. This is often described as a spanda or throb. It is not a true throb, as this implies some sort of movement in space, but is the perception of the Shiva principle.

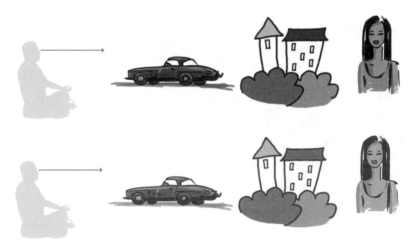

Technique 54

Fifty-four (Maya)

This is the play of consciousness that goes on in the world. It is often translated as "illusion."

In this technique you view all aspects of the manifestation, activity, time, worldly knowledge, desire, etc. as part of the totality. You see the divinity in all aspects of the world as-is, undistracted from the goal of enlightenment.

○ Ajna
● Anahata

○ Ajna
● Anahata

Technique 55

Fifty-five (Thoughts)

Be mindful of when desire arises and be careful to stop these thoughts. They are from the mind and cause fluctuations in it that are a hindrance to keeping it one-pointed. This is the same reason one feels happy after obtaining something one desires. The mind is fluctuating thinking about the desire, and once the desire is obtained the mind becomes still and your true nature (bliss) is revealed to a greater extent.

Desire is considered as a water element; thus, when breathing, it is associated with exhalation. If you pay less attention to this phase of the breathing then it will aid in dissolving strong desires.

With practice your mind will come under your control and desires will cease to arise. You should try and be mindful of removing the object of desire from your mind. For instance, it is all right to observe that your friend has a nice car, but one should be mindful of the thought, I want that car.

Technique 56

Fifty-six (Mindfulness)

You must develop the practice of viewing everything as part of the divine manifestation. The saint and the beggar, the gold and the mud, the friend and the enemy are all part of the same consciousness encompassing the totality. When the yogi is able to see god in the beggar, then he has realized the truth. As you see yourself in the mirror, so when you look at the phenomenal world, you should see only divinity.

Technique 57

Fifty-seven (Consciousness)

You begin to realize that your consciousness and your body exist separately. You will experience this in the dream and deep sleep states, but also in astral travel experiences. When you start to view your consciousness as all-pervasive and the same as everyone else, then the feeling of duality vanishes. You will come to realize that the same consciousness pervades the whole manifestation.

I am Tessa   I am Milind   I am Michael

O   Ajna

O   Ajna   Technique 58

Fifty-eight (I-consciousness)

Most people who have no awareness of the divinity refer to themselves as "I." This "I" represents the witnessing consciousness in all beings and should be observed. The people themselves are not using the "I" in this way, but the yogi realizes that there is only "I" and nothing else.

Technique 59

Fifty-nine (God)

Contemplate the fact that your essential nature is that of god. That does not mean you should develop a huge ego, as this denotes a lack of understanding of the true nature of the self. You should not view yourself as a limited being with birth and death, but rather as the eternal "I" consciousness.

Technique 60

Sixty (Intuition)

You will develop intuitive knowledge and experiences as you progress on this path. Initially you may ascribe them to coincidence, but after a while you will realize that you are obtaining intuitive knowledge. This is explained further in the section on intuitive experiences and signifies that you are attuned to the universe.

Additional Questions
And Answers

What should I experience in meditation?

During these sessions, you will gradually develop an awakening of the kundalini. You will have to try the different techniques numerous times to see if they work. Each individual is different and so you will find a technique that works very well for one person and not so well for another.

In general, I recommend that once you find a set of techniques that work, concentrate on those. The object of meditation is to make your mind one-pointed.

Usually when you start you will find that the mind tends to wander. This is normal. If it does then go back to counting the phases of breathing as in technique one. I have found this an excellent technique for developing one-pointedness. I have also found that it helps to use this as a starter technique prior to trying the more difficult techniques.

In the process of meditation, you may experience a buzzing sensation, or pressure or lights in any of the chakra areas. This usually indicates activity of the kundalini. When it first starts to occur there is a feeling of excitement in the mind, which tends to disrupt the experience. Over time you will be able to control this. Gradually the mind becomes very still and the breath becomes naturally suspended with no effort on the individual's part. Getting to a thought-free state requires a lot of sincere practice.

One should approach meditation as a daily activity with time allotted for it. Be careful not to allot token time so that the meditation can be ticked off like other activities or chores.

Also try and maintain a sincere disposition in the activity. Imagining that meditation will give you supernatural powers, enhance your personal magnetism or make you somehow mystical are thoughts that are better avoided. I would also stay away from bringing it up in casual conversation. The practice should be viewed as your attempt to see the divinity within yourself, with success measured by how well you see it in other people.

What is Samadhi (enlightenment/superconsciousness)?

This is the state where one is merged with the divinity. There are different stages of Samadhi. Once you are able to make your mind one-pointed and completely still, you have to drop the concept of trying to "reach" the Samadhi state. At this point any effort to meditate should be dropped and the yogi should just be. It is an effortless state. At this point your perception of yourself will disappear as you are merged with the divinity. At some point in the meditation you will "reappear." It is during this merger that you will obtain intuitive knowledge. The yogi cannot "know" this experience as it is a transcendental experience and the Truth cannot be "known." Knowing implies something that is finite, with name and form. The process of enlightenment will gradually progress to the point where the yogi is "experiencing" total bliss and non-duality in the waking state.

What is Intuition?

Once you are on a spiritual path and meditating regularly, you will start to develop intuitive experiences and knowledge. The intuitive knowledge usually comes after having intense meditative experiences. It comes in the form of subtle pointers and suggestions that arise in one's mind spontaneously. Initially you may think that they are fortunate coincidences, but as they keep occurring with more frequency over time, you will come to realize that it is the intuition at work.

How can I use Intuition?

I have found that as my meditation increased I could use intuitive knowledge to help solve not only my mundane daily problems, but also very difficult life problems. The way to do it is as follows: Firstly, you have to develop the capability of making your mind one-pointed during meditation. At this point your mind becomes very still and you are in a state of attunement. I like to think of it as attunement with the universe. Once in this state you should bring up your problem and drop it in the void. There should be no desire or judgment attached to it, and no solution that you have thought up using your own mind. Just drop the problem into the void in an egoless way and stop worrying. Usually the problem will solve itself in short order. This may sound too good to be true, but it has been my own experience and also that of everyone else I know who meditates regularly in our group. This can be used to make day-to-day life much less stressful.

How do I see God?

The process of meditation is to merge yourself back to the divinity. You cannot "see" god because that implies the existence of a duality. You, separate to god, having the experience of "seeing" god. The individual consciousness exists in every being and even insentient matter is a manifestation of the divine. You have to clear the filter that is stopping you from experiencing your own true nature. The filter is your mind, senses and intellect. The state has to be experienced and cannot be understood through words. It is a transcendental state above the level of thought.

What will happen when I die?

Your individual consciousness or Atma exists infinitely and will continue after your physical mind and body die. If you associate your "I" with your body and mind then you will not experience anything at death, as they will cease to function at that time. If you are associated with your Atma as your true self, then you will continue to exist.

Can I be a Christian, Jew, etc. and still meditate?

There is nothing in yoga that stops you having your own religious beliefs. The practices and experiences are designed to show you Truth. There is no dogma attached to it. Your experiences can be placed in the context of your religion as you like.

What is the experience of Shaktipat Diksha and Kundalini awakening?

I will describe my own experience of this event, although the experience varies from individual to individual.

Although I had grown up with book knowledge of meditation and yoga, it was only in 2000 that I started practicing in earnest with a daily meditation and pranayama. Over a two-year period I would meditate at night when the kids had all gone to bed and the house was quiet. I reached a point where I was at a plateau. During the meditation my mind was calm, but not one-pointed and completely still. I realized that I would need some help and contacted my parents, who lived in London. They were frequent visitors to India and had many learned people and swamis visiting them over the years. I had heard about one recently and inquired when he would be in London. Oh, he has gone on a two-year retreat, my mother informed me. My heart sank. Well, I could wait a little longer. She informed me that another lady swami was interested in giving talks in the US and could I set her up with one at UC Davis, where I had worked? I agreed. Several months later I picked up Swami Radhikananda, who had come from her yoga school in Pune, India, and drove her to my house. We chatted in the car about various philosophical topics until I found I had no more questions to ask. Somehow the answers she gave seemed to be the truth. There were no hedging or inconclusive answers and I had a feeling of peacefulness.

Once in the house she asked if I would like her to initiate my kundalini with a Diksha. I was a little shocked and didn't know what to say. I did not know if it would somehow tie me to this swami after I had planned to meet the one my parents knew. Also, I was unsure of what the experience would be, and frankly I was a little afraid. So I declined and she did not seem to mind.

The talk at UC Davis went well; she demonstrated the various hand mudras and showed how the breath changed with them. I had the experience along with some amazed audience members, although I also noted there were others who seemed very skeptical.

The night before I was to drive her to the airport to go back to Bombay, I was wracked again by the idea that I had declined the Diksha. What if she was sent to offer it to me? What if the chance never arose again? With these thoughts I timidly asked if she would initiate me and to my relief she said that she would do it the following morning prior to leaving for the airport.

At 5 AM we sat down to meditate. I had my usual experience of calmness, still lacking the something that I was hoping to get. She gently touched me with her thumb on my forehead and placed her hand on my head. My anticipation grew. Was I about to experience the ultimate state? I waited and relaxed, but nothing seemed to be happening. After several minutes she calmly asked me to open my eyes. It's done, she exclaimed. Nothing had happened.

I drove her to the airport wondering how to tell her that I had experienced nothing. I finally broached the subject and asked her what was meant to happen after a Diksha. She told me not to worry and that from now on when I meditated I should try and duplicate the experience. I didn't have the heart to tell her that nothing had happened. As I waved her off I was overcome by a deep sadness, as if I was saying goodbye to a beloved relative. I drove back though the high desert heading home and switched on the music.

The artist was Jimi Hendrix, a musician I had loved since my early teens. As I listened to the song I knew so well I was struck by how intense the music sounded and how nuanced the lyrics were. As I drove out of the high desert into the spruce-blanketed valley where we lived, I noticed a bluish haze I had never seen before. It seemed to be permeating the whole valley. As I drove closer I started to notice how green the trees looked. They were a brilliant, almost luminescent green. The colors of everything looked far more intense and brighter than I had ever seen them. As I came into town to meet my family and some friends for a craft fair, I began to be overcome by an intense feeling of bliss and happiness. We walked around the stalls as my whole being was overcome with this joy. I felt my individual self completely dissolve into the whole and I gazed on this marvelous play before me of which I was a part. All the while there hung about me this imperceptible bluish haze. I asked my wife if I seemed different and she replied I was my usual self. After arriving home in this state of total elation I sat down to meditate. Within minutes, all my closed eyes could perceive was an intense white light flooding the world inside my head. I bathed in the light for an hour. After the meditation I relaxed and the feeling of bliss gradually subsided. I had no doubt that I had experienced the non-dual state of Samadhi. I knew that the only reason I had had that experience was due to the Diksha. It was the most significant experience of my life and I had just placed the Swami on a flight to India!

Appendix

MUDRAS

Chakra: Sahasrara

Element: Beyond All Elements

Mantra: Silence

Chakra: Ajna

Element: Essence of All Elements

Mantra: (Guru) Om

Chakra: Vishuddha

Element: Space

Mantra: Hmm

Chakra: Anahata

Element: Air

Mantra: Ymm

Chakra: Manipura

Element: Fire

Mantra: Rmm

Chakra: Svadhishthana

Element: Water

Mantra: Vmm

Chakra: Muladhara

Element: Earth

Mantra: Lmm

CHAKRAS

● Sahasrara – Beyond Elements
○ Ajna – Essence of All Elements
● Vishuddha – Space
● Anahata – Air
● Manipura – Fire
● Svadhishthana – Water
● Muladhara – Earth

Suggested Reading

Singh, Jaideva. *Vijñ□nabhairava, Or, Divine Consciousness: A Treasury of 112 Types of Yoga.* Delhi: Motilal Banarsidass, 1979. Print.

Johari, Harish. *Chakras: Energy Centers of Transformation.* Rochester, VT: Destiny, 2000. Print.

Author Biography

Milind Dhond is a cardiologist practicing in Northern California. He has practiced Kundalini Yoga under the direction of Swami Radhikananda for the last fifteen years. He currently resides in Davis, California, with his wife and three children. Dhond is a Professor at UC Davis, and is a Sixth Degree Black Belt and Professor of Dan Zan Ryu Jujitsu. He is the Sensei of Green Valley Kodenkan in Cordelia, California, where he teaches Jujitsu and Kundalini Yoga.